Neil Chadwick was born and raised in the North West of England. During a 22-year career in the armed forces, he served both in the UK and further afield, before eventually settling in Lincolnshire with his wife, Cheryl. He has two daughters, Leanne and Zoe, and is a grandad to Joshua, Aimee and Olivia.

Neil Chadwick

RECOLLECTIONS

AUSTIN MACAULEY PUBLISHERS™

LONDON • CAMBRIDGE • NEW YORK • SHARJAH

A CIP catalogue record for this title is available from the British Library.

ISBN 9781398459038 (Paperback)
ISBN 9781398459045 (ePub e-book)

www.austinmacauley.com

First Published 2022
Austin Macauley Publishers Ltd®
1 Canada Square
Canary Wharf
London
E14 5AA

I would like to acknowledge the support of Joan, my mum; and Chuck, my late dad; especially my wife, Cheryl; and daughters, Leanne and Zoe, who have been instrumental in pushing me to submit my poems for consideration. Without them, it is unlikely the poems would have ever left the laptop.

I would also like to acknowledge the work of the publishers, without whom this book would not have reached publication.

A Watching Brief

I see a light, it's far away, but as I watch, it nears,
I recognise some friends I thought I'd lost, they look so clear.
They beckon me towards the light, I know not what to do,
So bright now here in my dark world, towards them I must move.

Then all at once, I'm in a room, I'm lying on a bed,
My family are all around, my wife, she strokes my head.
Whilst I look peaceful, those around have tears, I know not why,
Then it dawns on me, I am watching from a cloud up in the sky.

My friends and I were caught in a sudden roadside blast,
Nothing could be done, it all occurred so fast.
Brought back home, some slender hope, my injuries severe,
But I succumbed, I lost the fight, the thirteenth one that year.

So that was that, on this man's earth, I could no more remain,
With those I loved the most, it will never be the same.
I shout, 'I'm here,' but no one looks, they cannot hear my words,
I try so very hard, but can't make myself heard.

No longer will they see you, says a voice that I now hear,
However, you can often visit and they may feel you near.
You can't talk or touch or feel, no longer interact,
That's just the way it is, a sad, but brutal fact.

I leave my cloud, and make my move, to test what has been said,
I stand next to my wife and place my hand upon her head.
She shudders, then she turns, and stares into my eyes,
I scream out, 'Yes, it's really me.' But she can't see, despite my cries.

It's true, I can observe, but I can't communicate,
That's what the future holds for me, forever now my fate.
I'll devote myself to watching from my cloud up here above,
I hope perhaps that sometimes, they will feel my love.

For that's not dimmed, it shines so bright, it's just that none can see,
I hope that they'll feel something and I pray they'll know it's me.
For this is now my whole life's work. It's all that I can do,
To keep on trying day and night, to get my message through.

An Ode to Age

Birthdays come around each year. It makes some people sad,
They look back over younger years, to see just what they had.
Youthful looks, a taught backside. But what has it become,
Wrinkles on a worn-out face, beneath…a saggy bum.

Where once was youth, a change has come. They're rarely up past 10,
Some much prefer a peaceful night, so did it change, and when.
They say that life it does begin. When a certain age comes round,
But you got there some years ago, how depressing does that sound?

Age it truly upsets some. Really gets them down,
That beaming smile, the cheeky grin, more oft than not, a frown.
40, 50, even more. Should you really care?
You've still got all of your own teeth and most of your own hair.

What lies ahead in years to come? What to look forward to,
Bus pass, wrinkles, memory loss but just what can you do?
It's OK, you needn't worry. It's not a rocky path,
But things do get a little tricky when you can't get out the bath.

But yes, you have a little while. A few years on your side,
But just to confirm reality, you can never turn the tide.
You could do cosmetic to assist. A quick job with the knife,
But you will get old, things will drop off, that's just a fact of life.

Christmas Covid

Christmas is coming, but Covid's growing fast,
It won't be like the ones that we've had in the past.
But have you stopped to think, what Santa has to do,
To meet the Covid risk assessment and get to me and you.

We all know that Santa has a grotto far away,
But even he's not safe, from the Covid threat today.
His Covid risk assessment, showed some elves needed to go,
So whilst some still make presents, the others are furloughed.

Sanitisers feature at every workshop door,
And keep your distance stickers, are covering the floor.
The two-metre requirement is a challenge as you see,
The elves are only small, with the tallest just three feet.

They sanitise their tools and keep the gift-wrap clean,
They work through night and day, this tiny well-knit team.
To get toys made and wrapped, making sure that nothings missed,
Whilst checking all the time, the nice and naughty list.

Santa's sleigh is ready. It's confirmed as virus free,
Ready for the man in red, parked near the Christmas tree.
Santa's got a face mask, elves now sanitise,
The reindeers have to distance when they fly across the skies.

But this year, like all others, Santa sure will try,
To visit every household, for we all know why.
You will see it on the faces of every girl and boy,
As they unwrap on Christmas morning, that very special toy.

This year's been like no other, a test for everyone,
We will look back and think, when this virus has gone.
How Santa and his elves saved the Christmas cheer,
With his Covid-compliant, socially distanced, reindeer.

Dad

I was six years old, when I learnt, Dad wasn't coming home,
I did not understand at first, that we'd be on our own.
Dad always comes back home to us, what has changed this time,
Had I done something wrong, was the fault all mine.

Dad always wore a uniform and let me wear his hat,
But it was far too big for me. I do remember that.
Every time I wore it, Mum and Dad would laugh and laugh,
As I peeked out from underneath, walking down the garden path.

I remember in the summer, playing in the swimming pool,
Then squirting Mum, but blaming Dad, who always played the fool.
Laughter filled the garden, chuckles all around,
Squeaks and squeals and screeching as we tumbled to the ground.

Just after my sixth birthday, Dad had to go to away,
I was told that it would be a while, till he came back to play.
That made me sad, but Mum said we could do some special things,
But that all changed in just two weeks, when I heard the doorbell ring.

A tall man and a lady were stood outside our door,
My mum just started crying. I saw her tears fall to the floor.
So I gave Mum a cuddle, as that's what she did for me,
As I knew this made things better. It will be okay, you'll see.

But it didn't make things better. My cuddle didn't help at all,
I tried giving Mum my favourite doll, as she leant against the wall.
Nothing dried the tears, or stem the sobbing noise she made,
I didn't know what was happening, which made me so afraid.

Then Mum gave me a cuddle and squeezed me really tight,
I even slept in the big bed, with my mum that night.
In the days and weeks that followed, I saw Mum cry most days,
We did lots together, we shopped and walked and played.

As I grow up, Mum does her best, but I really miss my dad,
At least I have some memories. For that, I'm really glad.
I have a special picture of us all, which I hold dear,
And although my dad is sorely missed. I sometimes feel he's near.

Sometimes Mum still cries. I don't know if she'll get better,
She sits in the big armchair and just cuddles Dad's old sweater.
We often sit and giggle about the fun we had,
Recalling all the special times I had with Mum and Dad.

Although he's never coming home. I still sometimes wear his hat,
It fits a little better now, the years have seen to that.
I miss you, Dad. I really do. Much more than you will ever know,
But perhaps, you do, perhaps you hear, every time I tell you so.

Escape

I long for sleep to take me, to a land so far away,
Where I can spend some carefree hours, before another day.
No worries there to chase me. No doubts to pull me down,
A great big smile upon my face will chase away the frown.

I know that this brief respite, will be over far too soon,
The sun will rise into the sky and chase away my moon.
Reality will dawn once more, about this life of mine,
Alone and hungry, cast aside and all I have is time.

Everything I once did own, has vanished in the past,
The happiness that brought me joy, was never meant to last.
I had so much to live for, so many hopes and dreams,
But they all crashed around me. Destroyed my bright sunbeams.

The cause of this was simply six short months out of my life,
The result. No home or family. I lost a loving wife.
Just six months was all it took, to destroy all that I had,
No more I am called sweetheart. No more am I called Dad.

I get flashbacks to that place. Hear voices call my name,
See images of colleagues lying dead with others maimed.
My mental health it crumbled, like sand seeping through my hand,
I would never be the same once I left that distant land.

My rage got out of all control, hurt those I loved so much,
They fled and now it's been so long that I have just lost touch.
I hated what I had become. Despised myself inside,
I was so low, my mood so dark I hadn't any pride.

That was two long years ago. You'll see that I'm still here,
I still struggle with the voices, although now they're not as clear.
The flashbacks are less frequent. I never see them when I sleep,
That's why I pray for sleep to come and dry these tears I weep.

My dreams are a respite, a break from that grief,
At least in my dream world, I have welcome relief.
I relish the day when my dreams never end,
And I live out my days, with just dreams as my friends.

Fear

I'm waiting here, it's been so long, I cannot go outside,
I tried it once, but fear it came and ushered me to hide.
I tried again, tried really hard, to smell the summer breeze,
But fear it wouldn't let me, it just would not appease.

That was many years ago. I haven't tried again,
I just sit here, give in to fear, loneliness and pain.
I've tried to fight, to battle hard, to overcome my dread,
I'm told that I can win and beat those demons in my head.

I'm not sure how, my foe is strong, I find it hard to fight,
For fear is joined by darkness and they're blocking out the light.
I need to find a path, which leads me out of here,
But my path, it is a crescent, no escape for me I fear.

Friends and family tried to help, to give me their support,
But I rejected all of it, my life, was just too fraught.
They tried to banish darkness, to feed my mind with dreams,
But the darkness kept on telling me that nothing's as it seems.

So it came to pass that help dried up, my future now looks bleak,
I listen out for hope, a chance, but only darkness speaks.
It tells me that my friends have gone and I have been deserted,
My mind goes into overdrive, my senses are alerted.

I'm guided down to the darkest depths, from where there's no way out,
It matters not, I'm not in charge, of that there is no doubt.
I've lived my life, my soul is lost, there's no respite for me,
I now see fear and darkness, their faces full of glee.

They reach out and stroke my face, then guide me to a door,
They motion that I go inside and sit upon the floor.
Once sat, the memories flood by, charging through my head,
I see lots of things I've done, hear many things I've said.

Then suddenly it's dark again, there's nothing, not a sound,
I feel my eyes are closing and I slump onto the ground.
I've nothing left. I've given all, I've lost the fight at last,
Everything I once did have, has now become the past.

The support, help, assistance, has now been forced away,
The sun has set, the clouds have loomed, no more light of day.
So goodbye to all, you tried to help, but I lost the will to fight,
I give my thanks for what you tried, but now, my last goodnight.

Pride

I served my country boy and man, it ended in a blast,
My whole career is finished, it's now all in the past.
The weeks of treatment, surgery, has made me what I am,
You look at me, what do you see? A disfigured, broken man?

I once was proud, healthy, fit, the top amongst my peers,
Nothing seemed to trouble me; it's true I had no fears.
Invincible that's what we thought, nothing could us trouble,
Until that fateful day, when that bomb, it burst our bubble.

A blinding flash, a deafening noise, rubble all around,
As we drove past those IEDs, buried in the ground.
We later heard that we had driven through a laser beam,
This triggered both the IEDs that targeted our team.

Two friends killed, three others maimed, I was a lucky one,
Other mothers have to mourn a very young, dead son.
Today, when you look at me, tell me what you see,
Face contorted due to burns, a partial amputee.

Taunts and calls I hear each day, from those who just don't care,
Those that don't, they just walk by, trying not to stare.
They have no idea about my past. How proud I did once stand,
Serving Queen and country in distant foreign lands.

But now I'm judged on looks alone, half my arm has gone,
I'm sure they would think differently, if they had been the one.
But this is me, it's who I am, the rest is in the past,
It's with me now forever, and that's how long it lasts.

Sometimes I want the world to know, I want to scream out loud,
I may not look like you, but I am bloody proud.
I served my country, day and night, I made the sacrifice,
Unlike those who sneer and mock, I paid a higher price.

So do not judge on looks alone, stand and think a while,
It's not that I'm unhappy; it's just that I can't smile.
I may not look like others do, but am the same inside,
Disfigurement is plain to see, but you can't see my pride.

Fireworks

The winter months upon us now. The time of year I dread,
Especially the fireworks that thunder through my head.
They re-ignite the thoughts that I try to forget,
I want it all to stop…ENOUGH…I've paid my debt.

Many people love, the coloured flashing lights,
That explode way up high and are reflected in the night.
The bangs the pops the whistles. A wave of celebration,
But the noises take me back to when I served our fine great nation.

The fireworks that I endured, are locked inside my mind,
As even when I left that land, they didn't stay behind.
So when the bangs or pops or whistles sound outside my door,
I am often then found hiding by the sofa on the floor.

It's so hard to explain these feelings I endure,
The smell of burning, images so vile, return once more.
So vivid now I see them all, the scene is just horrendous,
I scream out loud as thick black smoke envelops all around us.

But then they're gone. It's quiet, but the sweat runs down my face,
I know the respite won't be long and I'll be back in that foul place.
It's so much worse this time of year, when others celebrate,
For me any many others, it's a time we've grown to hate.

Oft concern for animals is discussed this time of year,
With suggestions and advice on how to cure their fear.
The vets they cannot help me. The doctors try their best,
But the fireworks and all they bring, remain my greatest test.

Hope

I see the new day dawn, and the sun rise in the sky,
I see that same sun set again, at least the days been dry.
This same event that I have watched, at least a thousand times,
Will never lose its wonder, for me a wondrous sign.

It means I fight another day, when my future once was bleak,
I had 16 broken bones, a ruptured spleen, I was so weak.
They even asked the padre, to say some words for me,
No one thought that another sunrise I would see.

The bomb blast was intense, my injuries severe,
I was the thirteenth casualty, of the war that year.
No one thought I'd live, that to another life I'd pass,
As no one had survived such injuries resulting from a blast.

But I lived to fight again, although no more in that land,
My spleen has gone, my left leg too and also my right hand.
I'm still grateful for that chance, to carry on my fight,
When many others haven't, for them the last goodnight.

My life today so different. I now fight on alone,
Sadly I just couldn't work and so I lost my home.
I'm living on the street and find it difficult to cope,
Sometimes I feel so down, at least I still have hope.

For others, life was cut too short, their hope was torn away,
Unlike me they can't observe the dawn of a new day.
No more suns will they see rise, nor set as dusk appears,
Nothing ever brings them back, that heartache's real for years.

That's why I am so fortunate, though some may disagree,
They don't see the hope, just my disability.
But they haven't been through the fight that I have done,
They haven't faced the reaper who beckoned me to come.

His invitation I turned down. I didn't take that track,
If I'd have walked along that path, then there was no way back.
So here I am, a different person than the one before,
Some of me is missing and I now sleep upon the floor.

But I watch that sun rise in the morn, then watch it set once more,
I huddle in my doorway as the rain begins to pour.
I accept my life is basic, it's a life I wouldn't choose,
But on the plus side, you can see, I have little now to lose.

So hope will drive me on, supported by that sun,
If I ever lose that hope, then the sun it will be gone.
It may sound very simple, but that's what gets me through
The darker times, the memories, that threaten to consume.

As long as I can watch that sun and keep my hope alive,
Then I'll get by, I'll solider on, like the song 'I will survive'.
It could have been much worse for me, my friends and colleagues died,
Their hope is gone, their sun has set, for them no more sun rise.

I Need To

My leg is simply metal, one hand is gone for good,
It could have been much worse for me, and I know it could.
My friends they offer pity, they don't know how I cope,
My other colleagues cold and dead, at least I have some hope.

I am learning now to walk again, to cope with just one hand,
Other parts of me were widely strewn, across a foreign land.
You have to come to terms, adapt and overcome,
As if you simply fade away, life may as well be done.

You have to look ahead, to grasp each chance you see,
There is no going back, you really must believe.
But I agree it's hard, it's not an easy life,
But life is always filled with challenges and strife.

So please don't say 'you can't' and please don't ask me why,
When I want to board a plane and jump into the sky.
I'm still a human being, I've still got things to do,
But I'm still learning day by day, as all of this is new.

I could just give up, go downhill and take the easy choice,
But I'm alive, my life ahead, for that I should rejoice.
I accept that I have changed, some days more blue than bright,
But I need to carry on, and win my greatest fight.

So please don't offer pity, feel sorry or look down,
When you see me struggle, as I hobble round the town.
For me it's just a challenge that I have to overcome,
And one day you will look at me and see how well I've done.

I need to try, I need to push, those boundaries and limits,
It is vital that I try each waking hour, each precious minute.
To feel myself grow stronger, to push and achieve more,
To try and drown those images, of friends dead on the floor.

I have a second chance, I have to cope and learn again,
To do everything I took for granted, now I must retrain.
I could look back, dwell on the past, and let the demons win,
I can never let that happen, I can't, I won't give in.

It's Over?

I know that it is over, but it's still so clear to me,
I know that it is over, that I should now be free.
I know that it is over, and I'm back home at last,
But it isn't really over, I can't escape the past.

I'm told that it is over, ended years ago,
I'm told that it is over, that no more blood will flow.
I'm told that it is over, what does that really mean?
As it isn't really over, at least not in my dreams.

They tell me it's all over, no more friends will die,
They tell me it's all over, no more time to cry.
They tell me it's all over, how can they really tell?
I don't feel it's all over, I get flashbacks of that hell.

The war it is now over, everyone's returned,
The war it is now over, but some were maimed and burned.
The war it is now over, but for some still very real,
For those, it isn't over, the heartache they still feel.

Do you think it's over, like the politicians say?
Do you think it's over, as the media portray?
Do you think it's over, that peace is here today?
For me it isn't over, despite what they all say.

Convince us that it's over, and banish vivid dreams,
Convince us that it's over, tell us what peace means.
Convince us that it's over, we still live it every day,
None can convince it's over, no matter what they say.

For me it isn't over, the violent dreams so clear,
For me it isn't over, flashbacks from year to year.
For me it isn't over, although the years have passed,
Each day I cry, 'It's over, please make it end at last.'

Leaving the Light

I prayed this day would never come, prayed almost every day,
I asked for help and guidance, but none has come my way.
This darkness I've been fighting, the battle near its end,
Casualties left behind, my family and friends.

Every ounce of energy was focussed on this fight,
I've tried so very hard and summoned every drop of might.
Because of this my will grows weak, the bouts no longer fair,
The end now getting closer is more than I can bear.

I have to rally, try again, defeat this wicked foe,
But my strength just won't allow me to continue trading blows.
The darkness it's become too strong, I'm almost overwhelmed,
I feel I'm being dragged off course, wrenched from my own helm.

Life can be so very harsh, it's wicked, that's no lie,
It deals out the cruellest fates, but fight them you must try.
I tried to fight, I really have, but my opponent is so strong,
Once you tire, he is content, that victory won't be long.

My own life, it is worthless, despite what others say,
The battles lost, it's time for me to choose a different way.
I'll welcome in the darkness, invite it here to me,
It is the only way for me to break out and be free.

But darkness comes with a price, you go to it alone,
Sacrificing all you had, including family, friends and home.
Although I've nothing anyway, all of that's long gone,
I'm all alone. The future's bleak, my darkness is THE ONE.

It's time to go, my strength is lapsed, my dreams are simply shattered,
As I step out and leave the light. Nothing seems to matter.
The light regresses quickly, then someone calls my name,
The darkness, it just laughs out loud and tells me they're to blame.

I'm now so deep there's no way out, my life close to its end,
No chance to say goodbye, to family or friends.
All alone I left this world, with darkness as my guide,
So now for all eternity, there'll be darkness by my side.

Left Behind

Once I had a husband. My children had a dad,
Smiles and love they were abound. We were rarely sad.
We had 10 fantastic years, together man and wife,
Memories to cherish, two great daughters, what a life.

We all knew that deployments were a cross we had to bear,
Although for families left behind, these times felt so unfair.
Suddenly you're mum and dad and all that they stand for,
Washing, cleaning homework, tears. They all fall at your door.

We waved him off that Sunday morn, as the sun began to rise,
I tried so very hard to stem tears welling in my eyes.
I recall that day so clear, as if it happened yesterday,
Now just five short years ago, the 21st of May.

As the weeks wore on, the postman came most days,
To deliver letters, little gifts, bringing cheer along the way.
But even better were the weekly phone calls that we had,
When for a brief time, he could be a husband and a dad.

The world came crashing down, one early evening in mid-June,
We were waiting for his phone call, huddled in the living room.
The doorbell chimed, my eldest went. Is Mum in? I heard them say,
Then in walked the squadron welfare officer, with the female padre.

No explanation was required. I knew exactly what this meant,
It's the news no loved one wants, when partners overseas are sent.
An incident two hours ago, two roadside IEDs
My husband's team were targeted. He's not coming home to me.

The numbness it was instant. I simply couldn't speak,
My daughters started crying and my knees became so weak.
I stared straight at the padre and I simply uttered why?
She had no explanation, but held my hand and I just cried.

I had no idea what to say, where to start, what to do,
The padre offered her support and said I'm here for you.
The rest is just a blur, of tears and grief and pain,
The dark place I was taken to, can't be visited again.

The challenges we faced, were insurmountable it seemed,
We had to re-evaluate, all our hopes and dreams.
Five years on the pain remains. Still hard to comprehend,
That fateful day I lost my lover, husband and best friend.

My daughters sometimes struggle and tears well in their eyes,
We often chat about him or to his photo on the side.
We only now have memories, to brighten up our day,
At least we still have those and they can guide us on our way.

Memories

I sat alone and listened to the screams and shouts she made,
Nothing else was in my head, she sounded so afraid.
I closed my eyes, but it got worse, please make him go away,
We thought that he had gone last week, but he returned today.

Then suddenly the shouts they stop, the screaming does subside,
That is usually my clue, to run away and hide.
'Where are you?' I hear the growl, doors slamming as he goes,
I curl up small now knowing, I'm another of his foes.

I'm coiled so small, but frightened, hoping me he will not find,
As if he does, I know, that once again he'll not be kind.
I've experienced his belt, his fists, a lighted cigarette,
Mum could never stop him, and she got so upset.

It changed today, when Mum attacked the man who hurt me so,
She told him it was over, that he would have to go.
Then he did shout, and my mum ran, he followed up the stairs,
We both were really frightened, but he just did not care.

He dragged her to the bathroom, the bolt I heard it slide,
I couldn't help, the door was locked and time for me to hide.
I knew that once he had some time, for me he'd start to track,
And once found, I would experience, thick welts upon my back.

I screamed when the hand touched me. I shouted in that place,
Then I looked up and saw it was a smiling policeman's face.
Relief was overwhelming, I was safe at last,
Time to see my mum again; it's now all in the past.

But I never saw my mum again, she never came back home,
I'm now with a new family, but still feel so alone.
My cuts have healed, my burns have gone, but memories are raw,
I don't think I will forget, those evil things I saw.

The day I said goodbye to Mum, they'd let him come to pray,
She couldn't even have that peace, upon her final day.
He smiled at me; I looked away, my hatred pure and clear,
I now have my life sentence; he'll be free in just eight years.

Middle Age

You know you're getting old when your knees begin to creak,
You feel a little grumpy, and your bladder's getting weak.
The aches and pains more frequent. Some wrinkles you now find,
The memory's not as it was, are you losing your mind?

Once up the stairs, two at time, you could bound and leap,
Now by mid-day the eye lids droop, it's time to have a sleep.
Now news at 10 past your bedtime, of that there is no doubt,
Not long ago it was the time you were ready to go out.

You used to sleep right through the night, nice and peaceful too,
But now at least three times a night you're visiting the loo.
The bladder's not as once it was, perhaps it has just shrunk,
You will just have to face the facts; you're no longer such a hunk.

Your youth is just a memory, the six pack it is gone,
Hair receding, thin on top, no longer number one.
What can you look forward to, getting plastic teeth?
Losing muscle function, they'll even liquidise your tea.

Old age it is around the corner, zimmers or a stick,
Perhaps electric scooters, then you'll be really quick.
People don't believe your age, that makes you feel much better,
Then you spoil it all by slipping on the grandfather style sweater.

You'll have to face it; age is something everyone does fight,
But it does creep up on you, when sleeping late at night.
When once awake you notice that the years have advanced so,
But is it really something that should make you feel so low?

The worries of your youth have gone, older, wiser, too,
And anyway it's not that bad, you're not yet 52.
There's still a spring within your step, a twinkle in your eye,
And you still manage to keep all of your underwear bone dry.

No Test for Me

The streets have been my home for nigh on seven years,
But this year brings along, a different type of fear.
Businesses are closed, so my source of food dried up,
My guitar no more results in coins flicked into my cup.

When previously the greatest threat was loneliness and cold,
There is now a deadly virus, or so I have been told.
You don't hear much news when you're living on the street,
Just pick up bits and pieces from the people that you meet.

Someone told me that my cough was sounding worse once more,
That my breathing was more laboured than they had seen before.
I do get short of breath, as I'm moved along once more,
To find another doorway with a reasonably dry floor.

I'm told there is a test that you can book online,
But I don't have such access, and haven't for some time.
No mobile to make a call, no cash to use the phone,
So how am I to book a test existing on my own.

Who will call for help if I continue getting worse?
Who will check that I'm alright and, for once, put me first?
How will I get the GP to call me back to chat?
I am not registered anywhere, so there is little chance of that.

When I am found, just hours later, it's far too late to act,
Another homeless person lost. That is a woeful fact.
Eventually all on my own, I will finally lay to rest,
But not included in statistics as I never had a test.

On Reflection

I look at the reflection, but don't recognise my face,
Try to recall the life that I once had, before this place.
Once young and fit. I knew no fear. The life was mine to live,
Now old and gaunt looks back at me, I've nothing left to give.

The eyes which once so bright and blue, have simply lost their shine,
The stubble mottled black and grey. My appearance marked by lines.
The smile that once adorned that face, has since been wiped away,
A few short weeks created this reflection here today.

I throw stones into the water. They disturb what looks at me,
But it's soon back, time and again, to remind me what I see.
Why don't I walk away, erase the beast before my eyes?
I can't. I'm just transfixed. I want to prove that it's all lies.

For a few short moments, the image that I see is wiped away,
But it reforms to mock me, time and again today.
I turn away, but feel its stare. I have to scrutinise,
Every line, scar and scratch I need to analyse.

I visually dissect, each and every pore,
Before I throw another stone, to disrupt the view once more.
I hope that when the ripples end, the vision will transform,
But when I check, I see it still. It makes me so forlorn.

I've visited this place, each day for three long weeks,
But I've never found that image that I desperately seek.
I pray I'll see it just once more to remind me of good times,
Of all those hopes and dreams that I've now left behind.

Each day I travel further to find those stones I need,
I have to dig them from the ground, which makes my fingers bleed.
Every splash I engineer, a wish that things will change,
That I will see my past again when my features re-arrange.

I know what the conclusion is before the water clears,
The truth in my reflection, now wet from my own tears.
I hope that soon the sun will ensure this pool does drain,
My reflection gone until the rain creates it once again.

Panic Stations

The weather forecast seems to show that snow is on the way,
That temperatures will plummet, Jack Frost will come and play.
So cancel trains and buses too, close the schools right now,
Buy crampons for your shoes, rent a 4x4 with plough.

Stock up on the rations, oh yes, and pile the water high,
We have to be quite quick before the white stuff comes from high.
Pack the car with shovels, consider snow chains too,
Just in case you can't get home, pack the porta loo.

Buy as much de-icer, as you can carry home,
Ensure you have a charger and a working mobile phone.
Check the weather forecast, the snow will soon be here,
It will be worse than anything, for many a long year.

But I am ready for the blast. I can almost last a week,
With the additional equipment, that I went out to seek.
Now it's just a waiting game, the sky it looks so dark,
The snow is nearly here, soon to make its mark.

Is that a flake…oh no it's started. Disaster, what to do,
I'm feeling cold, I need some soup and then perhaps a brew.
Eyes fixated on the sky…it looks a little brighter,
But I'm sure the temp is dropping, should my scarf be tighter.

Oh look, there is the sun, the dark clouds disappear,
The snow, it didn't come too much, no more need to fear.
The precautions, now not needed, perhaps another day,
When the dark clouds come with old Jack Frost and he begins to play.

Season's Greetings?

It is the season of goodwill, or so the story goes,
It's so cold, my hands are numb, there's no feeling in my toes.
I see the twinkling coloured lights, I hear the Christmas chimes,
I used to love this time of year, till I fell on hard times.

I used to love that morning, Santa's magic all around,
Delighted squeals, excited voices, presents were abound.
Hearty food, always too much, friends knocking on the door,
The sound of wrapping paper being scrunched upon the floor.

Those moments, now just memories, in my mind, so far away,
I'm jolted to the present, back to how I live today.
I like to linger in those thoughts, of warmth and love and lights,
It's better than reality, each day, I live a fight.

A daily battle to find food, the struggle to stay warm,
The same challenge day to day, for me it's now the norm.
I see you look and judge me, herd the children far away,
Don't get close, don't walk near, go a different way today.

But I am a human being, I have wants and needs like you,
My wants and needs are basic, just some warmth and food will do.
I once walked in your shoes, and thought the thoughts you think,
Avoided homeless people, their problems caused by drugs or drink.

Mostly self-inflicted, often look a dreadful state,
But are they all responsible, the authors of their fate?
From a personal perspective, that's often just untrue,
I don't relish, or enjoy, being sat in front of you.

I was serving Queen and country, in a sunny distant land,
Had two daughters I adored and a wife to hold my hand.
But I returned, completely changed, scarred in soul and mind,
The love, the warmth and happiness, to it all, I was so blind.

Our relationship fragmented, of course blame laid elsewhere,
But looking back into the past, the blame's all mine, not theirs.
But it's too late to build those bridges, too much water's flowed,
Resigned to the loss of family, no more hands to hold.

I look unkempt, one to avoid, I don't blame you at all,
When you walk by and stare at me as I sit by this wall.
I see the thoughts behind your eyes, the same that I once had,
I wish that I could reassure, not all of us are bad.

This time of year more challenging. I recall what once was mine,
Season's greetings sent to all, they bypass me this time.
Laughter, love and family, appreciate it all,
Even the tacky baubles that decorate the hall.

You don't know what the future holds, I never dreamed of this,
The tacky baubles, eccentric gifts, all I really miss.
But history is written, now new chapters they await,
I hope that in those chapters, love conquers over hate.

Tell My Story

I oft sat there and wondered, where did it all go wrong?
All alone, just with my thoughts, somewhere I don't belong.
My downfall was dramatic, in just a few short weeks,
I found myself in that dark place, a long way from my peak.

I only have to look back, just eight short months ago,
When I first caught sight of that land, 2000 feet below.
No one knew what waited, in the heat and dust beneath,
But in our own abilities, we had infinite belief.

That belief was sorely tested as the weeks rolled by,
But that belief was torn apart when our first comrades died.
What had happened, we weren't sure, confusion all around,
Time simply stood still, bewilderment abound.

The sudden thunderous noise, the flash attacked your eyes,
The plume of smoke and debris, sent rising to the skies.
'Man down,' came the shout. 'Medic,' was the cry,
My colleagues torn apart, to save them I must try.

Through the smoke and debris, I tore across the ground,
Avoiding metal fragments, scattered all around.
What met me was horrific. Ingrained now in my mind,
Never in my wildest dreams could I imagine what I'd find.

The devastation total, the scene looked so surreal,
All my sensations numb, I knew not how to feel.
I had to treat them now, three injured friends of mine,
Their injuries severe and there was little time.

I tried everything I knew, worked like a man possessed,
But knew that my success, would be a greater test.
Despite all of my efforts, and everything I tried,
I watched with devastation as my three colleagues died.

One by one they passed away, my assistance not enough,
I tried my best to help them, but their loss, it was so tough.
As the weeks wore on, demeanours changed, dark clouds appeared,
The flashbacks came more frequent, much worse than I had feared.

My outlook grew much darker, my solace became drink,
I started going off the rails, as I got to the brink.
One day I took the final step and went into freefall,
Career in tatters, future bleak, my help too far to call.

The flashbacks turned to nightmares, each one so real and bright,
Reliving all I couldn't do, each and every night.
The hopeless feelings so intense, cut deeper every time,
My thoughts were overtaken, the blame was solely mine.

At the depths of my despair, I ended on the streets,
Begging just to live, searching bins for food to eat.
I now look down from up above, to see me lying there,
The medals on my chest, atop this prose for all to share.

It will tell the story of my life and all my challenges and woes,
That will now be read by all. It's how my story goes.
So as I drift away from here, to what my future holds,
I hope that you will understand, now that my story's told.

The Footballer

The football season's here again, the matches on all screens,
But every time I watch them play it makes me want to scream.
The Prima Donnas prance around, they're paid an awful lot,
But if they dare get tackled, you'd think that they'd been shot.

A football pitch? Not anymore. The catwalk seems more apt,
Socks pulled high above the knee, just part one of the act.
Hairstyles cost more than I earn. Sponsorship abound,
But if they dare get tackled, they collapse onto the ground.

Rolling round, screams and shouts. The end of a career?
The referee waves and play goes on. No free kick? Oh dear.
So up he jumps and off he sprints, a whole 400 yards,
Remonstrates with the referee, to encourage his use of cards.

But the referee is stoic and the cards remain unused,
The player can't believe it and he looks so confused.
Review the footage, VAR, the captains now embroiled,
He wants some justice for his team as so hard have they toiled.

The referee accedes, to shouts and wagging fingers,
He knows that peace will not be his, until with VAR he lingers.
40 seconds later, the decision now complete,
A yellow card for diving. He was nowhere near your feet.

I want a VAR review of the referee's decision,
I am a prima donna and can't be treated with derision.
Petition FIFA, change the rules. I demand a meeting,
I don't deserve a card, just because I got caught cheating.

Once the dust has settled, 90 minutes at an end,
The prima donnas leave. Although by now, they're all good friends.
But only till the next time that the first half starts again,
Then all they want to do, is pretend that they're in pain.

The Forgotten Fight

The festive time is always linked with glee and festive cheer,
But it won't be the same this time. No joy for me this year.
I still listen to the carols and see the coloured lights,
Memories will stir once more and I'll recall delight.

A memory is all it is. I no longer join the Christmas crowds,
The lights are now so dim and the songs are not so loud.
The coloured jumpers, fresh mulled wine, the Santas and their sleighs,
Are all the things that I enjoyed, before that fateful day.

That fateful day preceded by a fateful afternoon,
Whilst deployed on operations on the 17th of June.
A routine town patrol, no different from the rest,
The beating sun and searing heat, severe enough a test.

The explosions loud and brutal. One left another right,
One colleague's death was instant, three others faced a fight.
Survival is a battle, many challenges to face,
Before you reach the other side. A calm and quiet place.

I stayed resolute and strong. Dug in to face the fight,
I tired so very hard, just to resist my harshest plight.
The struggle was one sided. My chance of victory so slim,
I had to try and stand up strong, but the light was growing dim.

My battle it was long. Ups and downs through every day,
The troughs and peaks, I met them all, head on, along the way.
But then the troughs got deeper, the peaks were barely there,
My chances of success no more than slight. It wasn't fair.

Despite all of my efforts, the end was soon in sight,
The darkness shrouded all around. The day fell into night.
Each route to my escape, was closed off one by one,
The last door slammed tight shut and my future it was gone.

'Another veteran lost', reads the front page big and bold,
As underneath it clarified *'just 26 years old'*.
By tomorrow, newer headlines will report a different plight,
My memory forgotten, just another forgotten fight.

The Journey

I sit and wonder, as the sun, climbs high into the sky,
Just what will come my way today, as I watch time pass by.
I look back, into my past. And smile at memories,
No resemblance at all, to the person you now see.

Now unrecognisable, from the man I used to be,
The reflection in the window, I don't identify as me.
The weeks and months alone, have left a telling mark,
My home comprises cardboard, near the toilets, in the park.

It wasn't always like this. I had a perfect life,
Two wonderful young daughters. A devoted, loving wife.
I'll now share my journey with you. But please don't be surprised,
If you observe some teardrops, welling in my eyes.

It's only four short years ago, but seems like yesterday,
That we packed up, made our plans, and soon were on our way.
We bid farewell to those we loved and tried to hide the pain,
But secretly we prayed, that we'd all come home again.

We knew the risks that faced us, the challenges severe,
Six months of work, trials and tests, then we'd be out of here.
The journey more demanding, than anybody thought,
The day-to-day assignments, became increasingly more fraught.

The heat, it was incessant. Sweat dripped from every pore,
The IEDs a constant threat that chilled you to the core.
One day it all became too real. The blast that killed and maimed,
The devastation total. Things would never be the same.

In six long months, I lost two friends. But that was just the start,
During the next two years, the love leaked from my heart.
My wife she needed something more. My daughters simply scared,
Frightened by their father. I know, it sounds absurd.

But the flashbacks came to haunt me. I screamed out in my sleep,
My tolerance was smashed apart. My regression was so deep.
They had to leave. They had no choice. Their safety paramount,
My brain possessed, or so it seemed, compassion had seeped out.

Support was there to help me, but the voices told me no,
My wife and daughters now at risk. They knew they had to go.
Suicide did tease me. It called me once or twice,
I was in a dark and lonely place. It wasn't very nice.

I was discharged six months later, which was followed by eviction,
I spiralled out of all control, lost courage and conviction.
So now I've shared my journey. I hope you understand,
My predicament was borne out of a visit to that land.

A decorated veteran, with my medals shining bright,
No other light in my dark life, as I now say good night.
My journeys at its end. I've reached a cul-de-sac,
Nothing left to live for. No more turning back.

The Smile

You see my smile and wonder, why my joy is clear to see?
I ask you pause a while, take some time, listen to me.
You will hear a story full of grief, of challenges and woes,
But there's much more to this smile of mine, and so my story goes.

You see a down and out, living rough here on the street,
My clothes are torn, my hair unkempt, shoes hardly fit my feet.
My bed, it varies nightly, depending where I roam,
Last night the shelter in the park, the place that I called home.

This has been my life now, for almost seven years,
Each day a growing struggle, but please don't shed your tears.
You see fortune shone upon me, and I'll share my tale with you,
Perhaps then you will understand the face that smiles on through.

My story starts some years ago when I was young and strong,
The forces life it beckoned and I was keen to join that throng.
The friendships grew, bonds matured, always there for one another,
We grew as close as family, I saw them like my brothers.

In just one moment, this all changed, my life turned upside down,
As we patrolled in close-knit form, outside that foreign town.
The shots they came from nowhere, bouncing all around,
We took cover where we could, some laid flat upon the ground.

This was shortly followed by a blinding flash of light,
A roar so deafening, smoke so thick, that day turned into night.
There my recollection ends, my memory wiped clean,
I lay there bleeding on the floor with members of my team.

In less than three short minutes, six young lives were torn apart,
Which led to friends and loved ones having hope ripped from their heart.
My survival was a lottery I could not expect to win,
But fortune shared its luck, stopped me sinking, helped me swim.

Recovery was long and hard, I learnt to walk once more,
I've lost one arm, my facial burns now mean my sight is poor.
The future with my brothers, just a memory in my past,
In time I lost my job and home. It was just too good to last.

Which brings me to the present day, now that you've paused a while,
You will need an explanation for this eternal smile.
It's not that I am joyful, or happy with my plight,
But at least unlike some others, I can continue with this fight.

So back again to the smile, which you see adorns my face,
It makes me look so happy, despite time spent in this place.
The smile is fixed, there is no change, the scarring sees to that,
That's why, despite this life, I smile like the proverbial Cheshire cat.

Time to Go

I sit here now, all on my own, where once was joy and glee,
Please stop a while, while I recount, what did become of me.
I wasn't bright, or clever, but neither was I bad,
But now my eyes are dull, my smile is gone, I feel so sad.

A servant of my country, that's what I used to be,
So proud to wear the uniform, over air and land and sea.
None could have predicted, for me what lay ahead,
Evicted from my house, a cardboard box to lay my head.

A forces veteran's what I am, but what do you really see,
A down and out that you avoid, or one prized for gallantry.
Medals did adorn my chest, a decorated man,
But then it all went sadly wrong, it wasn't in my plan.

I served my stint, but it was hard, I lost good friends of mine,
All of them, they went too soon, taken in their prime.
Like others I did struggle, to come to terms with what I'd seen,
Injured, dying all around, were members of my team.

I didn't want to go, I had to leave, I couldn't stay,
But when I walked out of those gates, it was a fateful day.
I was told support is out there, but for it I still await,
The support that I was used to, is back inside those gates.

I struggled for employment, my health it faded fast,
Nightmares came more vivid, my future's now my past.
Stony broke, without a job, I couldn't pay the rent,
The landlord said he understood, but was it really meant?

It mattered not, as two weeks later, his empathy no more,
Out on the streets, I turned around and watched him lock the door.
I thought I'd hit rock bottom, I'd really lost my way,
I had to sell my medals, I despised myself that day.

Now three months later, nothing's changed, I'm still without a home,
I have no money, friends or hope, I'm simply on my own.
I oft look back to who I was and what I have become,
The shame is overpowering, just what could I have done?

Promotion, moving through the ranks, some stripes upon my arm,
Supervising those beneath, with an air of calm.
But all that's gone, those hopes and dreams, I never will fulfil,
My dreams were torn apart, for me it's all uphill.

All this ruined, blown apart, scattered like my friends,
There's nothing left to live for, my life is at its end.
I look ahead, the blackness looms, there isn't any light,
It's time for me to say goodbye, farewell. To all goodnight.

Two Sides to Every Story
The Chief Executive

I am the chief executive, the leader of the pack,
I steer this good ship, business, and keep it right on track.
My managers appreciate my strong and stable lead,
To my suggestions they all listen. My advice they heed.

Remunerated nicely, in a comfortable way,
Ensuring those beneath are heard, but don't really have a say.
Responses to my surveys contain suggestions from the floor,
I pass them off as mine to get awards fixed to my door.

We invest in all our people, even have a charter mark,
Receive plaudits for the landscape within our local park.
The twitter feed is rampant, the Facebook site well liked,
I even have a charging station for my electric bike.

Those that work the shop floor, appreciate my role,
For without me they would be lost, with most left on the dole.
Revered I am for leadership, direction and support,
Without me, the employees' life would be immeasurably fraught.

So it's with an air of satisfaction that I review my role,
Personal success the aim, my one and only goal.
Those that work the shop floor, ensure that I achieve,
And in my leadership ability, they all, as one, believe.

The Employee

I am the office worker that has to smooth the way,
To ensure the business prospers, and there is no delay.
The orders need to be on time, production smooth as silk,
All the workers employed here, working at full tilt.

But the chief exec has sent another bloody survey,
Completion it is compulsory, by end of work today.
This will set our process back, another pointless task,
Stupid worthless questions is all he seems to ask.

Do you feel invested in, do you like our charter mark?
Nobody could give a toss about the landscape of the park.
Other than the kids whose skate park was ripped up,
To enable the new landscaping with the fountain in the cup.

It achieved another green award, a shield upon the door,
Of the chief exec's office, high up on the fourth floor.
Most here don't know who he is, he is just 'the boss',
If he ever visited our shop floor, it would be because he's lost.

His focus solely on awards, certificates and shields,
Investing in his people, words are cheap we feel.
Investing in the CEO is what he is about,
He doesn't listen to our calls, even though we shout.

Why Me

I am feeling rather sleepy. I know it won't be long,
Before I drift away once more, it feels so very wrong.
I'm looking down a tunnel. There's a bright light far away,
It seems to move away from me, it's just too far today.

I lie here on my own. No friends or family near,
I hear voices in the distance, there are people coming near.
'Oh my god,' I hear the cry. I didn't see her there,
My body feels so broken, and blood seeps throughout my hair.

I feel a hand upon my face. A noise in my head, humming,
Then rapid footsteps I can hear, somebody is running.
A second set of footsteps into the distance run,
I now feel some deep sharp pain, but most of me is numb.

I hear a car stop next to me. 'Phone help,' the frantic shout,
A quiet voice, 'You'll be okay,' but I can hear his doubt.
Now I'm cold despite his coat. Another voice is here,
But it sounds so very far away and it is now unclear.

Darkness it envelops me. It won't be long I know,
I hope it's to a better place that I will have to go.
I don't know why that driver felt he had to leave me there,
Just looking after number one and I don't think that's fair.

I hope one day he will reflect, on what he did to me,
I hope that in his conscience he never will be free.

Winning

You visit and listen to my story, pause a while,
You visit and you listen as I recall the darker times.
You visit and you listen whist I get it off my chest,
I'm so grateful that you listen, it makes my burden slightly less.

You know I find it painful when I talk about that place,
You know I find it painful as the tears stream down my face.
You know I find it painful to relive my grief again,
I'm so grateful that you sat here to help relieve my pain.

The darkness, it does haunt me, each and every day,
The darkness, it does haunt me, I fight to clear the way.
The darkness it does haunt me, it worsens in the night,
I'm so grateful for your words, you help the world seem bright.

I fight to rid myself of this, the hateful dreams, so clear,
I fight to rid myself of this, now into its fourth year.
I fight to rid myself of this, it just keeps coming back,
I'm so grateful for your guidance, you help me find another track.

I feel I'm making progress, and will face my foes head on,
I feel I'm making progress, but the job is not yet done.
I feel I'm making progress, but it will take a while,
I'm so grateful that my progress is supported by your smile.

This journey's not been easy, but support has pushed me on,
This journey's not been easy, but we've come through as one.
This journey's not been easy, the challenges severe,
I'm so grateful as without you, I would have lost within a year.

The future's looking brighter and I can smile once more,
The future's looking brighter, no more darkness at my door.
The future's looking brighter, I can see that now so clear,
I'm so grateful for a future and for having you so near.

I'm proof they can be beaten, and banished from the door,
I'm proof they can be beaten, and cross your path no more.
I'm proof they can be beaten, banished from your life,
I'm so grateful that I beat them with the love from my dear wife.